The Amazing Itty Bitty Book of QuickBooks® Shortcuts

15 Quick Tips for Faster Data Entry into QuickBooks®

Whether you are just getting started using QuickBooks® or are a veteran at your trade, you are likely looking for ways to streamline the tedious task of data entry. In this book you will learn simple ways to make your data entry efforts easier, your records more accurate, and your job more fun.

Questions I hear repeatedly:

- "Isn't there an easier way?"
- "Why can't I find what I am looking for after I enter it?"
- "How can I keep my desk cleared from all this paperwork?"

If you want to be more efficient, more accurate, and more confident in your job, pick up a copy of this helpful book today!

Your Amazing
Itty Bitty® Book of
QuickBooks® Shortcuts

*15 Simple Tips for Quicker Data Entry
Into QuickBooks®*

Barbara L. Starley, CPA
Certified QuickBooks® Pro Advisor

Published by Itty Bitty® Publishing
A subsidiary of S & P Productions, Inc.

Printed in the United States of America

Itty Bitty Publishing
311 Main Street, Suite D
El Segundo, CA 90245
(310) 640-8885

ISBN: 978-1-931191-52-4

Dedication

This book is dedicated to all of the entrepreneurs and small business owners I have had the opportunity and pleasure to serve - as their CPA, mentor, and friend - as well as those who I have yet to meet.

Stop by the Itty Bitty website to find interesting blog entries regarding QuickBooks®:

www.IttyBittyPublishing.com

For more information check out Barbara's website at:

www.BarbaraStarley.com

Table of Contents

Introduction

Introduction

In this Itty Bitty Book you will find 15 simple tips for quicker data entry into QuickBooks® that will help you:

1. Streamline your data entry efforts
2. Make fewer mistakes, and
3. Eliminate wasted time.

It all starts with learning where to go to find what you need and remembering a few simple keystroke combinations.

Although all of the steps contained herein are written from the perspective of the desktop version of QuickBooks® - specifically QuickBooks® Pro - you will find most of the information is useful for quicker data entry into QuickBooks® Online as well.

Simple Tips for Quicker Data Entry into QuickBooks®

Shortcut #1
There's No Place Like Home

If you are looking for a great visual depiction of the accounting process in a flowchart format, look no further than the QuickBooks® HOME screen.

1. Your HOME page is custom-made just for you based on the preferences you set for your company.
2. Your HOME page is divided into 5 main sections with each section showing several clickable icons.
3. Many of these pictures are linked by arrows showing how the work flows through the accounting process.
4. The HOME page serves as the place for quick access to a variety of useful functions within QuickBooks® without having to find those links on various dropdown menus.

Let's Check Out Your HOME Page

See if you can find these commonly accessed links:

- Vendors (Top Section)
  - "Vendors" = Vendor List
  - Enter Bills
  - Pay Bills
- Customers (Middle Section)
  - "Customers" = Customer List
  - Create Invoices
  - Receive Payments
- Employees (Bottom Section)
  - "Employees" = Employee List
  - Enter Time
- General (Top Right Corner)
  - Chart of Accounts
- Banking (Bottom Right Corner)
  - Record Bank Deposits
  - Reconcile Accounts
  - Write Checks
  - Check Register
  - Enter Credit Card Charges

Note: The HOME page of QuickBooks® Online shows a graphical picture of your finances rather than the accounting process.

Shortcut #2
Don't Touch That Mouse

Reaching for the mouse every time you want to move around QuickBooks® is by far the biggest time waster I see people make when they are doing data entry. Why? Because:

1. It simply takes longer to move your hand away from the keyboard to grab your mouse and move back into position on the keyboard again.
2. Your chances of making mistakes increase significantly when you use your mouse, because it's very easy to skip important points of data entry when you grab the mouse.
3. When data is entered incorrectly or is missing altogether, you waste precious time trying to find transactions which would have been easy to locate if you simply would have left the mouse untouched.
4. Using the TAB key (or Shift + TAB, if you want to move backwards) will eliminate many common input errors because it gives you a chance to consider each field of data entry.

Prevent Errors. Use TAB instead of the mouse.

Many of the mistakes that are made in QuickBooks® are actually quite easy to prevent by simply using TAB (or Shift + TAB if you want to move backwards). Here are just a few of the errors that you can avoid:

- Wrong Check Number
- Incorrect Transaction Date
- Memo Carryover From Prior Entry
- Missing Information
- Lack of Detail in Accounting

Shortcut #3
Plus & Minus

You might think that the plus and minus keys are only important for adding and subtracting, but when it comes to data entry in QuickBooks®, there are other powerful uses for these two arithmetic keys:

1. "+" increases the check number
2. "-" decreases the check number
3. "+" adds a day to the date field
4. "-" subtracts a day from the date field

Let's practice what you've learned so far.

From your HOME page, in the bottom right-hand corner of the screen, you'll see the "Banking" section. Click on the Write Checks icon to pull up a blank check.

- Step 1 – Verify your bank account. You want to make sure that you are going to deduct the amount of the check from the appropriate bank account.
- Step 2 – TAB to the check number field.
  - If you are recording a check you wrote manually, enter the check number in this field.
  - If you used your debit card, type "debit" in the check number space.
  - If you paid an invoice online, you can type "online" in this field.
- Step 3 – TAB to the date field. Depending on the preference that is set, your QuickBooks® program may default to the current date or to the date of your last entry. Let's assume that it defaults to today's date, but you wrote this check two days ago. Because you tabbed to the date field, the date should be highlighted and all you need to do is hit the "-" (minus) key twice to move the date back 2 days.

Shortcut #4
"T" is for Today

This little shortcut is one of my favorites. Whenever you are at a date field, and the date is highlighted, simply hit the "T" key and the date will automatically be adjusted to Today's date.

You might be surprised how often you use this little keystroke shortcut. Try it for yourself when entering dates on just about any form, including:

1. Checks
2. Bills
3. Invoices
4. Sales Receipts
5. Customer Payments
6. Payroll

Other Handy Date Shortcuts

Other date-related shortcuts that may come in handy, but will likely be used less frequently, include:

- "Y" = beginning of the current **Y**EAR
- "R" = end of the current YEA**R**
- "M" = beginning of the current **M**ONTH
- "H" = end of the current MONT**H**

Shortcut #5
Intuit® = Intuitive

You don't have to be a fast typist to be quick at
data entry in QuickBooks®; but it is helpful to be
able to look at the screen as you type - rather than
watching your fingers as you hunt & peck around
the keyboard. QuickBooks® will try to "guess"
what you are looking for – whether that is a
customer, vendor or account name. Here's an
example of how this works:

1. Let's say that you met a client at
   Starbucks® for breakfast. As you begin
   to enter the expense in QuickBooks®,
   you'll start typing in the Payee name as
   "S-t-a-r."If you are watching your screen,
   QuickBooks® may have already
   assumed that you are looking for
   Starbucks and all you need to do is TAB
   to accept the guess and move on to the
   amount field.
2. Same thing happens in the Account field;
   you can start typing "M-e-a"….and
   QuickBooks® will likely pick up "Meals
   & Entertainment" as the account choice.
   Since this is correct, simply TAB to the
   next field.

Bonus Tip!! Deductible business meals & entertainment expenses must identify:

- Date of meeting. This is indicated on the check or credit card charge screen.
- Where you met. This is the name of the Payee on your check or credit card charge.
- Amount of expense. This is also indicated on the check or credit card charge screen.
- Business purpose of meeting.
    - Use the memo field next to the amount of your breakfast to identify the business purpose of your meeting.
    - You might write something like, "Breakfast with Mary Adams, XYZ Co., re June marketing plan."

Why I recommend memos:

- These notes will come in very handy if you are ever audited. Three years from now, you probably won't remember who you were with or why you were meeting.

Shortcut #6
From Beginning to End

One of the luxuries of QuickBooks® is to have some data automatically load into certain fields. For example, if you set up your vendor record properly (see Note below), your account number will automatically appear in the memo field of a BILL or a CHECK. This is a great feature because, of course, you want your vendor to give you credit for your payments by applying your payment to your account. You may also want to add a specific invoice number to that memo line; in which case, you will love this Home/End shortcut.

1. HOME takes you to the beginning of a line.
2. END takes you to the end of a line.

Note: The Account Number field is found on the Payment Settings tab of the vendor record.

Let's Continue With Your Training.

- In Shortcut #3, we were moving around a blank check using the TAB key, and I suggested you use your "+" and/or "-" key to adjust the check number and date. As you continue to TAB through the spaces, you will enter the Payee Name and Amount of the check.
- Remember: Don't touch that mouse to find the Payee Name. Simply start typing the vendor name and QuickBooks® will intuitively try to find the name you are looking for.
- TAB to the memo field. Your account number should already be there and should be highlighted. Hit your END key to move your cursor to the end of the line and simply enter the specific invoice number(s) you are paying.

Why is this important?

- Using memos is important because you do not want your vendor applying a payment to an invoice you are disputing. By identifying the invoice number, you retain control of how a payment is to be applied.

Shortcut #7
Account Numbers are Old School

Unless your tax accountant requires that you use a specific numbering system for your Chart of Accounts, I can't think of any good reason to use a numbering system in your QuickBooks® file; but I see clients who have "always done it this way" and are convinced that they can enter data faster using numbers. I can't think of a single time where this has proven to be true. Instead of account numbers, simply use words to describe the account – such as:

1. "Office Supplies" to categorize, well, office supplies; or
2. "Telephone" to categorize telephone expenses.
3. Isn't that a whole lot easier than having to remember that "5250" is "Dues & Subscriptions"?

Setting the preference for account numbers:

If you absolutely, positively, must use account numbers, then be sure that the account number does not become part of the actual Account Name by following these steps:

- Go to "Edit" at the very top left side of your screen.
- Click on Preferences on the drop down menu.
- Click on Accounting on the left scroll bar.
- Click on the Company Tab
- Check the box to "Use Account Numbers."

Using these same steps, the preference can be easily turned off later when you realize that the numbering system is no longer useful.

When is your numbering system no longer useful?

- When you run out of account numbers.
- You run out of sub-account numbers.
- Your accounts are out-of-order alphabetically.
- You realize that using words is simply a better option.

Shortcut #8
When in Doubt "Ask My Accountant"

As you are entering data in QuickBooks®, you may come across an item or two that you simply have no idea what it is. You have three choices:

1. Guess
2. Save it for later
3. Use "Ask My Accountant"
       (See Note below)

Note: In QuickBooks® Online and in the older versions of QuickBooks® Pro, this account is called "Uncategorized Expenses".

If You Guess:

- You may guess wrong.
- You'll have to remember where you guessed it should go.
- You may have to find the transaction and make corrections.

If You Save It For Later:

- Your bank/credit card balance will not be accurate, because you'll have unrecorded transactions.
- Depending on your version, you may not be able to download additional transactions.
- You won't be able to reconcile your bank account.

If You Post It To "Ask My Accountant":

- You have a specific holding place for questionable items.
- You know where to find the transactions when you get the answers you need.
- Your bank balance will be accurate.
- You can reconcile your bank account.
- You will know what questions need to be asked before you print your financial reports for your boss, your bank or your tax accountant.

Shortcut #9
Insertions & Deletions

Imagine spending time entering a long, multi-line estimate or invoice for a customer and realizing that you missed a line up towards the top. Or, conversely, you may need to delete a line from a multi-line transaction - but who wants to leave a gaping space on the form? This can be so frustrating. Take a deep breath and remember these two little shortcuts:

1. Control + Insert
2. Control + Delete

To Insert A Line:

- Set your cursor on the line just below the line that you want to insert.
- Hold down the Control Key and hit the Insert Key.
- A line will open up above the line you are on.
- Add the missing information.

To Delete A Line:

- Place your cursor on the line you wish to delete. Hold down the Control Key and hit the Delete Key.
- The entire line will be deleted in one quick entry.

Shortcut #10
Memorize It!

Memorizing transactions can save you a lot of
data entry time. Did you know that you can
memorize just about any type of transaction?
Here are just a few possibilities:

1. Recurring monthly bank charges
2. Automatic charges to your credit card
3. Monthly rent invoices to tenants
4. Quarterly insurance payments
5. Monthly automatic transfer to savings
6. Annual subscription renewals

How to Memorize a Transaction:

- Begin by entering the transaction for the current period.
- Before leaving the transaction, hold down the Control Key and hit the "M" Key. [Ctrl +M = Memorize]
- At this point, a pop-up window will appear and you'll have some decisions to make about the transactions that will get entered in the future:
  - Automate Transaction Entry?
  - How Often?
  - Next Date?

Shortcut #11
Name of the Game: Consistency

If you really want to streamline your data entry, start by getting consistent with how you name everything in QuickBooks®, including:

1. Vendor Names
2. Customer Names
3. Employee Names
4. Account Names
5. Bank Account Names

Naming Recommendations:

- Proper Names: Show as Last Name, Full First Name
- Company Names: Eliminate "The" from the Vendor Name
  - You can always add "The" to the corporate name in the address field, and
  - You can specify in the vendor record how the name should be printed on the check
- Employee Names: Set the Preference to show "Last Name First" on reports.
- Account Names: Combine similar types of accounts by using "sub-accounts"
  - Never post to the "header" account if there are sub-accounts available
  - Only use sub-accounts if the additional breakdown is useful
- Bank Account Names:
  - Include the Bank's name
  - Indicate the type of account
  - Add the last 4 digits of the account number or debit card associated with the account
  - Example: BofA-Checking 5422

Shortcut #12
Use Bank Feeds

As online banking has become more popular, I believe that both QuickBooks® and the banking industry have improved the process and the security of connecting and downloading banking and credit card transactions directly into QuickBooks®. Before using the time-saving feature of bank feeds:

1. Be sure you feel comfortable with the security of the connection between your bank and QuickBooks®.
2. Be careful that you do not double-up on entries by downloading or otherwise recording duplicate entries.
3. Don't get sloppy. Take the time necessary to properly record and allocate transactions as they are entered to avoid the time-consuming task of finding and correcting data-entry mistakes.
4. Be sure you understand the costs associated with this feature. Some banks assess a monthly fee for the "Direct Connect" service, but allow "Manual Downloads" for free.

How To Set Up Bank Feeds:

- From your Chart of Accounts, highlight the account you want to setup for Bank Feeds.
- Double-click to bring up the register for the selected account.
- At the top of the register, click on "Setup Bank Feeds."
- QuickBooks® will run the Bank Feeds Wizard which consists of the following steps:
    - Step 1 – Find your bank.
    - Step 2 – Connect your bank to QuickBooks® by entering the User Name and Password you would use if you went directly to your bank's site.
    - Step 3 – Decide which connection you prefer: Direct Connect (fees may apply) or Manual Download/Web Connect (usually free).
    - Step 4 – Link the bank account to the appropriate checking or credit card account in your QuickBooks® file.

Shortcut #13
Beware of Renaming Rules

Don't be too hasty in your quest to finish your data entry that you allow renaming rules to apply to all transactions indiscriminately. As you begin to enter your Bank Feed transactions (see Shortcut #12), be aware of the "fine print" on each new, downloaded transaction. With each entry, you get to decide whether to:

1. Agree with the renaming rule, or
2. Ignore the renaming rule.

When to Agree with Renaming Rules:

- When the downloaded name is descriptive enough to allow you to know that the Payee you connect to it will be consistent from one transaction to the next.
- When the expense account attached to the Payee is consistent from one transaction to the next.

When to Ignore Renaming Rules:

- When the downloaded name is not descriptive enough for you to know who the Payee is without looking closer at the transaction.
- When the amounts may be categorized differently from transaction to transaction.

Shortcut #14
You Are In Control

I'm not a big proponent of trying to remember a lot of keystroke combinations, but I use the following commands so often, I had to share them with you:

1. Ctrl + A – **Account List**
   No matter where you are in QuickBooks, you will be able to see your Chart of Accounts with this command.
2. Ctrl + D – **Delete an Entire Transaction**
   Be careful – this is a powerful & irreversible command. Word of caution: Never, ever delete a reconciled transaction without guidance from an expert.
3. Ctrl + W – **Write Checks**
   Because almost all transactions that reduce your bank balance are recorded as a check, this command can come in quite handy when you want to quickly get to the Write Check screen.
4. Ctrl + F – **Find**
   This is the ultimate search command.

Let's Try Using The "Find" Command:

Think of your QuickBooks® file as a huge box full of data and you want to funnel that data down to one particular entry. Hold down the Control Key and hit the "F" key. Be sure you are on the Advanced Tab and set the Filter(s) to search by one or more of the following:

- Amount
- Date
- Name
- Number

Once the system has isolated the transaction(s) that match your criteria, you can quickly "Go To" the transaction to obtain further information.

Shortcut #15
Ditch the Calculator

If you still have a calculator sitting on your desk, taking up space, get rid of it. Did you ever think you'd hear an accountant tell you to ditch your calculator? You simply don't need it – or if you do, it's rare; so free up some space on your desk and use one of these two methods to do your calculating:

1. Click on EDIT at the top left corner of your screen; scroll down to "Use Calculator". You can minimize the calculator so you can easily pull it up anytime you need it from your icon tray.
2. Anytime you are at an "amount" field, you can quickly and easily make a calculation. Simply type a number into the amount field, and as soon as you use one of the arithmetic operands (+-*/), QuickBooks® will assume you want to make a calculation. Use your TAB key to "accept" the result of your calculation.

When You Are Dealing With Accounting, There Are Amount Fields Everywhere, Including:

- Checks: Amount of the check, as well as the detail amounts
- Invoices
- Deposits
- Bills
- Journal Entries

Let's Give It A Try. Let's assume you want to pay two invoices on one check:

- Step 1 – Hold down your Control Key and hit the "W" to bring up a blank check.
- Step 2 – TAB to enter the check number, date, Payee, then move to the amount field.
- Step 3 – At the amount field, enter the amount of the first invoice, hit the "+" key, and you'll see what looks like a calculator register tape. Type in the amount of the second invoice and hit your TAB key to accept the result of your calculation.

You've finished. Before you go…

Tweet/share that you finished this book.

Please star rate this book.

Reviews are solid gold to writers. Please take a few minutes to give us some itty bitty feedback on this book.

ABOUT THE AUTHOR

Barbara Starley is not your typical CPA; she doesn't do income taxes or day-to-day bookkeeping. As a Certified QuickBooks® Pro Advisor, Barbara built her own entrepreneurial enterprise and knows what it takes to construct a business that you love.

As an author, speaker and trainer, Barbara speaks the language of the small business owner. As your "On-Call Controller," she is great at simplifying complex accounting and tax issues and turns confusion into confidence.

Whether one-on-one (on-site or virtually) or in a webinar or seminar format, Barbara comes alongside entrepreneurs to guide, mentor and empower them – primarily in the areas QuickBooks® set-up, training & troubleshooting.

By bridging the gap between the small business owner's in-house staff and outside advisors, Barbara creates a win-win-win scenario. The owner wins because they feel informed and can be more proactive with their business finances; the outside tax preparer can give better tax advice because they receive good, solid financial records; and the in-house staff wins because they feel empowered and confident in their job.

For more information check out Barbara's website at www.BarbaraStarley.com

If you enjoyed this Itty Bitty® book you might also enjoy…

- **Your Amazing Itty Bitty® IRS Tax Audit Prevention Book** – Nellie Williams, EA

- **Your Amazing Itty Bitty® Business Tax Book** – Deborah A. Morgan, CPA

- **Your Amazing Itty Bitty® Book of QuickBooks® Shortcuts** – Barbara L. Starley, CPA

- **Your Amazing Itty Bitty® Little Black Book of Sales** – Anthony Camacho

- **Your Amazing Itty Bitty® Video Marketing Book** – Gary Howarth

- **Your Amazing Itty Bitty® Safety Book** – Stephen Charles Carpenter

Available online